TIM BATTY

PowerKiDS
press™
New York

Published in 2023 by The Rosen Publishing Group, Inc.
29 East 21st Street, New York, NY 10010

Originally Published in English by Haynes Publishing under the title: *Dinosaurs Pocket Manual* © Haynes Publishing 2019

Cataloging-in-Publication Data

Names: Batty, Tim.
Title: Meat-eating dinosaurs / Tim Batty.
Description: New York : PowerKids Press, 2023. | Series: Dinosaur discovery | Includes glossary and index.
Identifiers: ISBN 9781725338456 (pbk.) | ISBN 9781725338470 (library bound) | ISBN 9781725338463 (6 pack) | ISBN 9781725338487 (ebook)
Subjects: LCSH: Dinosaurs--Juvenile literature. | Carnivorous animals--Juvenile literature. | Carnivorous animals, Fossil--Juvenile literature.
Classification: LCC QE861.5 B38 2023 | DDC 567.912--dc23

Design: Richard Parsons and James Robertson

Picture credits:
Cover: DM7, HitToon, John Archer, kzww, Valentyna Chukhlyebova
De Agostini/NHMPL: 3, 4-5, 8-9, 22-23, 24-25
Barislav Krzic/NHMPL: 3
NOPPHARAT7824: 30-32
John Archer: 2-3
John Sibbick: 12-13, 28-29
Chris Srnka: 3, 6-7, 10-11, 14-15, 16-17, 18-19, 26-27
Tim White/NHMPL: 20-21

Manufactured in the United States of America

CPSIA Compliance Information: Batch #CSPK23. For further information contact Rosen Publishing, New York, New York at 1-800-237-9932.

The Author

Tim Batty was educated at the University of Wolverhampton before entering on a career in museums. He is a "founding father" and curator of The Dinosaur Museum in Dorchester, UK, and his favorite dinosaur is Iguanodon – its fascinating story and past first sparked and inspired his fascination with dinosaurs.

Contents

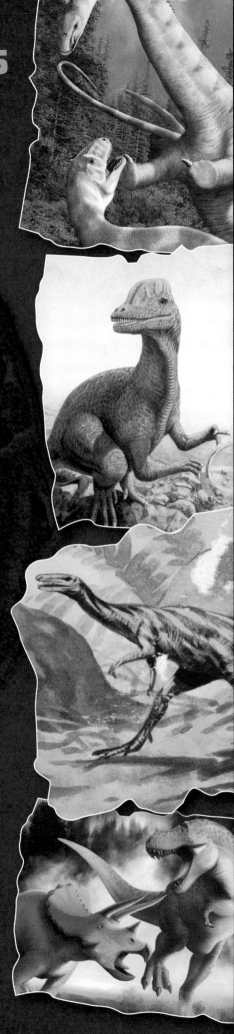

About This Book

This exciting book is packed with everything you need to know about carnivorous, or meat-eating, dinosaurs, including stunning pictures, fascinating facts, and all the vital statistics. It features 11 species of dinosaurs, from the notorious *Tyrannosaurus rex* to the awesome *Allosaurus*.

Allosaurus

Pronounced: *AH-loh-saw-ruhs*

Allosaurus was one of the first giant theropod dinosaurs of the Late Jurassic period and a top predator. Many fossils have been discovered in the United States, where it would have preyed on larger plant-eating dinosaurs. It was a fierce hunter, biting into its prey with its sharp, backward-curving teeth. *Allosaurus* used its powerful neck to create a hacking motion with its head. Its skull was designed to withstand a huge impact. Sauropods may also have been part of its diet, especially if *Allosaurus*es hunted in small packs of two or three. *Apatosaurus* bones have been found with teeth marks from an *Allosaurus*. The legs of the *Allosaurus* were sturdy, with sharply clawed feet, but the speed at which it could run would have been limited by its size. Some skeletons have been found with bone injuries, possibly caused by falling during the chase. Its skull was about 30 inches (80 cm) long and had a characteristic small bony ridge above each eye socket, measuring more than 2 inches (5 cm) high and 4 inches (10 cm) long.

Statistics

Meaning	Different Lizard
When	Late Jurassic
Time	154–144 million years ago
Max length	40 feet (12 m)
Max height	15 feet (4.6 m)
Max weight	6,615 pounds (3,000 kg)
Stance	Biped
Where	United States (Colorado, Utah, Wyoming), Portugal & Tanzania
Diet	Carnivore
Activity	Hunting, possibly in small packs
Intelligence	Medium
Named by	Othniel Charles Marsh
When named	1887
Order	Saurischia (Lizard-hipped)
Type	Theropoda, Tetanurae, Carnosauria

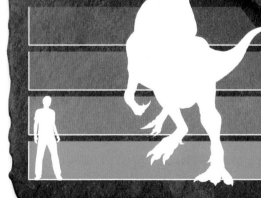

Timeline
Million Years Ago

Late Cretaceous	99–66
Early Cretaceous	144–99
Late Jurassic	159–144
Middle Jurassic	190–159
Early Jurassic	205–190
Late Triassic	227–205
Middle Triassic	242–227
Early Triassic	251–242

Baryonyx

Pronounced: *beh-ree-OHN-icks*

Baryonyx is different from most other theropods in several ways. The elongated skull is much like that of a crocodile in shape, and the neck is straight. The jaws contain 96 serrated teeth, which are rounded in cross-section rather than flattened. The gigantic 10-inch (25 cm) long claw bone on the three-fingered hand distinguishes *Baryonyx* from other dinosaurs. *Baryonyx* was mainly a two-legged animal, but possibly walked on all fours some of the time. The jaws and teeth, and the finding of fish scales from the fish *Lepidotes* in the rib cage, indicate that *Baryonyx* ate fish rather than meat, although it probably scavenged meat as well. It lived on land, along the banks of the rivers or swamps, probably hunting in a similar style to bears today. William Walker, an amateur fossil hunter, discovered the large claw bone in 1983 at a clay pit in Surrey, England. The new dinosaur was named *Baryonyx walkeri* after its distinguishing feature and the person who found it.

Statistics

Meaning	Heavy Claw
When	Early Cretaceous
Time	127–121 million years ago
Max length	33 feet (10 m)
Max height	15 feet (4.5 m)
Max weight	4,400 pounds (2,000 kg)
Stance	Biped
Where	England
Diet	Carnivore
Activity	Hunting along riverbanks
Intelligence	Medium
Named by	Alan Charig & Angela Milner
When named	1986
Order	Saurischia (Lizard-hipped)
Type	Theropoda, Tetanurae

Timeline
Million Years Ago

Late Cretaceous
99–66

Early Cretaceous
144–99

Late Jurassic
159–144

Middle Jurassic
190–159

Early Jurassic
205–190

Late Triassic
227–205

Middle Triassic
242–227

Early Triassic
251–242

Carcharodontosaurus

Pronounced: *car-CAIR-oh-don-toh-saw-ruhs*

Named after the great white shark, *Carcharodontosaurus*'s teeth were triangular and serrated along both the front and back edges, and up to almost 8 inches (20 cm) long. Many fossilized teeth have been found and it seems that *Carcharodontosaurus* continually shed and replaced teeth, as many dinosaurs did. Like *Baryonyx*, it most likely ate fish, as well as hunting large plant-eating dinosaurs, including sauropods. The first remains of *Carcharodontosaurus*, discovered in the 1920s in Egypt, were destroyed by bombing during World War II. It was not until 1996 that Paul Sereno discovered the remains of a second *Carcharodontosaurus* in Morocco. He found a skull and a few associated bones. The skull proved to be larger than *Tyrannosaurus rex*'s, at about 5 feet (1.5 m). A close relative of *Carcharodontosaurus* is the massive *Giganotosaurus*, which is known from South America. Africa and South America were joined, right up until the beginning of the Cretaceous period, so these two dinosaurs likely shared a common ancestor.

Statistics

Meaning	Shark-toothed Lizard
When	Cretaceous
Time	112–94 million years ago
Max length	46 feet (14 m)
Max height	13 feet (4 m)
Max weight	16,000 pounds (7,200 kg)
Stance	Biped
Where	Egypt, Morocco, Tunisia, Algeria, Libya & Niger
Diet	Carnivore
Activity	Hunting
Intelligence	Medium
Named by	Ernst Stromer
When named	1931
Order	Saurischia (Lizard-hipped)
Type	Theropoda, Tetanurae, Carnosauria

Timeline
Million Years Ago

Late Cretaceous
99-66

Early Cretaceous
144-99

Late Jurassic
159-144

Middle Jurassic
190-159

Early Jurassic
205-190

Late Triassic
227-205

Middle Triassic
242-227

Early Triassic
251-242

Carnotaurus

Carnotaurus is only known from one almost complete skeleton found in Patagonia, Argentina. It was a strange-looking theropod with a large head but a short snout, giving the dinosaur a face like a bulldog. This feature and the two heavy horns over the eyes give *Carnotaurus* its name. Despite this large, strong head and neck, the lower jaw was light and weak, showing that it might have scavenged for food. The horns were most likely used by males when competing for mates, just like deer do today. *Carnotaurus* had very short, weak arms, the purpose of which is not known. The arms were shorter even than those of *T. rex*, a very distant relative. Along with the skeleton, a large skin impression of the right side of the dinosaur was recovered. This showed that *Carnotaurus* had a scaly, reptilian type of skin composed of a mosaic of small, non-overlapping scales arranged in rows over the body.

Statistics

Meaning	Meat-eating Bull
When	Late Cretaceous
Time	84–65 million years ago
Max length	25 feet (7.5 m)
Max height	13 feet (4 m)
Max weight	2,200 pounds (1,000 kg)
Stance	Biped
Where	Argentina
Diet	Carnivore
Activity	Scavenging or hunting
Intelligence	Medium
Named by	Jose Bonaparte
When named	1985
Order	Saurischia (Lizard-hipped)
Type	Theropoda, Ceratosauria

Timeline
Million Years Ago

Late Cretaceous
99-66

Early Cretaceous
144-99

Late Jurassic
159-144

Middle Jurassic
190-159

Early Jurassic
205-190

Late Triassic
227-205

Middle Triassic
242-227

Early Triassic
251-242

Ceratosaurus

Pronounced: *see-rah-toh-SAW-ruhs*

Ceratosaurus had two brow horns or ridges above the eyes and a large horn on the snout. That's where its name comes from. The horns were probably used for display purposes when competing for a mate. Unusual for a theropod, it had a jagged crest of small bony plates running the length of its neck, back, and tail. Their purpose is not known. Both *Allosaurus* and *Ceratosaurus* remains have been found in the Dinosaur National Monument in the United States, and in Tendaguru in Tanzania, making them rivals for the same food sources. *Allosaurus* was the larger and more developed animal and would have had the advantage. *Ceratosaurus* was a primitive theropod and exhibited two unusual features: it had four sharply clawed fingers on each hand instead of the usual three, and its tail was flexible. More advanced theropods had tails that were stiffened by tendons to give balance, and because of this they are classified as tetanurans. It is likely that *Ceratosaurus* hunted in small packs, preying on small or young dinosaurs.

Statistics

Meaning	Horned Lizard
When	Late Jurassic
Time	154–144 million years ago
Max length	20 feet (6 m)
Max height	10 feet (3 m)
Max weight	2,850 pounds (1,300 kg)
Stance	Biped
Where	United States (Colorado, Utah), Tanzania
Diet	Carnivore
Activity	Hunting
Intelligence	Medium
Named by	Othniel Charles Marsh
When named	1884
Order	Saurischia (Lizard-hipped)
Type	Theropoda, Ceratosauria

Timeline
Million Years Ago

Late Cretaceous	99-66
Early Cretaceous	144-99
Late Jurassic	159-144
Middle Jurassic	190-159
Early Jurassic	205-190
Late Triassic	227-205
Middle Triassic	242-227
Early Triassic	251-242

Dilophosaurus

This strange-looking dinosaur takes its name from the pair of large, curved bony crests on each side of the head. After the first discovery of three skeletons in 1942, it was wrongly identified as a new species of *Megalosaurus*, because the skulls were poorly preserved. In 1964, Samuel Welles returned to the site and discovered a fourth specimen, which clearly showed the two crests. The dinosaur was renamed *Dilophosaurus* in 1970. The crests were fragile and probably just for display purposes. Not all the skeletons have been found with crests, so they could be a feature of the males. Its head was large, with strong jaws and sharp teeth. *Dilophosaurus* would likely have captured, killed, and torn up its prey with its claws. Otherwise, it would need to scavenge food, as its teeth were too weak to kill a struggling dinosaur. Like *Ceratosaurus*, the hands had four fingers, three of which were usable, while the fourth was very small. *Dilophosaurus* most likely hunted in packs, when they were not scavenging off carcasses of dead dinosaurs.

Statistics

Meaning	Two-ridged Lizard
When	Early Jurassic
Time	202–190 million years ago
Max length	20 feet (6 m)
Max height	8 feet (2.5 m)
Max weight	1,100 pounds (500 kg)
Stance	Biped
Where	United States (Arizona), China
Diet	Carnivore
Activity	Hunting & scavenging
Intelligence	Medium
Named by	Samuel Welles
When named	1954
Order	Saurischia (Lizard-hipped)
Type	Theropoda, Ceratosauria

Timeline
Million Years Ago

Late Cretaceous
99-66

Early Cretaceous
144-99

Late Jurassic
159-144

Middle Jurassic
190-159

Early Jurassic
205-190

Late Triassic
227-205

Middle Triassic
242-227

Early Triassic
251-242

Gallimimus

Pronounced: *ga-luh-MIH-muhs*

Gallimimus was the largest of the ornithomimidae, or ostrich dinosaurs. It differed from its American cousins, such as *Ornithomimus* and *Struthiomimus*, chiefly in the shape of the skull. Its head was long and thin, with a toothless beak similar to that of a bird. Its eyes were large and faced sideways. Its body was relatively small, with a long neck, which held the head above the body in the classic ostrich style, and the tail was long. *Gallimimus* was covered with downy feathers, not suitable for flight, but good for insulation, and with longer feathers on the arms. Its long legs had hollow bones, making them lightweight but strong and giving *Gallimimus* the ability to run quickly, probably as fast as a modern ostrich. *Gallimimus* was mainly a carnivore with a diet of small reptiles, mammals, and insects, but it would also have eaten fruits and seeds, and maybe eggs. Its only defense against larger meat-eating dinosaurs was its speed. It was one of the fastest dinosaurs, reaching speeds of up to 35 miles (56 km) per hour.

Statistics

Meaning	Chicken Mimic
When	Late Cretaceous
Time	71–65 million years ago
Max length	20 feet (6 m)
Max height	7.5 feet (2.3 m)
Max weight	1,000 pounds (450 kg)
Stance	Biped
Where	Mongolia
Diet	Omnivore
Activity	Hunting or grazing
Intelligence	High
Named by	Halszka Osmólska, E. Roniewicz & R. Barsbold
When named	1972
Order	Saurischia (Lizard-hipped)
Type	Theropoda, Tetanurae, Coelurosauria

Timeline
Million Years Ago

Late Cretaceous
99-66

Early Cretaceous
144-99

Late Jurassic
159-144

Middle Jurassic
190-159

Early Jurassic
205-190

Late Triassic
227-205

Middle Triassic
242-227

Early Triassic
251-242

Giganotosaurus

Pronounced: *jai-GAN-uh-tuh-saw-ruhs*

In 1993, when *Giganotosaurus* was discovered, it took the record from *Tyrannosaurus rex* for being the largest meat-eating dinosaur. It was a massive beast, with a skull that was 6 feet (1.8 m) long. However, its brain was smaller than *T. rex*'s. The jaws were full of shark-like teeth up to about 8 inches (20 cm) long, which were designed for slicing through flesh rather than crunching bones, as in the case of *T. rex*. It was a powerful dinosaur, with arms that were short and strong and with three-fingered hands and claws. Typically, as with most large theropods, the legs were sturdy and not built for running fast, and the feet had three main toes with a much-shortened fourth toe. *Giganotosaurus* most likely preyed on the large sauropods that lived at the same time. A skeleton of one was found near the remains of *Giganotosaurus*. It would have needed to hunt in small packs to kill an adult sauropod, but on its own, *Giganotosaurus* could kill an injured or young sauropod.

Statistics

Timeline
Million Years Ago

Meaning	Giant Southern Lizard
When	Early Cretaceous
Time	112–99 million years ago
Max length	45 feet (13.7 m)
Max height	16 feet (5 m)
Max weight	17,600 pounds (8,000 kg)
Stance	Biped
Where	Argentina
Diet	Carnivore
Activity	Hunting
Intelligence	Medium
Named by	Rodolfo Coria & Leonardo Salgado
When named	1995
Order	Saurischia (Lizard-hipped)
Type	Theropoda, Tetanurae, Carnosauria

Late Cretaceous
99-66

Early Cretaceous
144-99

Late Jurassic
159-144

Middle Jurassic
190-159

Early Jurassic
205-190

Late Triassic
227-205

Middle Triassic
242-227

Early Triassic
251-242

This big, heavy-bodied dinosaur moved on two powerful legs. It was a typical large theropod, with three main toes with sharp claws (plus the trace of a fourth toe) on each foot. At the end of each short, strong arm was a three-clawed hand. The head was large, about 3 feet (1 m) in length, and supported by a strong, S-shaped neck. The long jaws held curved, saw-edged teeth flattened from side to side. The long tail balanced the weight of the body as it moved. Unique tracks of *Megalosaurus*, discovered in Dorset, England, and on display in The Dinosaur Museum, shows a tail-drag impression. This demonstrates that on occasion *Megalosaurus* walked with its tail on the ground. It was an excellent hunter, attacking large plant-eating dinosaurs, including some sauropods. *Megalosaurus* is an important dinosaur because it was the first one to be scientifically described and named. This first description was based on a jawbone. The very first dinosaur remains, a thigh bone, had been discovered by Robert Plot in 1676 and wrongly identified as belonging to a giant human! Richard Owen later recognized this as another example of *Megalosaurus*.

Statistics

Meaning	Great Lizard
When	Middle Jurassic
Time	180–169 million years ago
Max length	30 feet (9 m)
Max height	10 feet (3 m)
Max weight	2,200 pounds 1,000 kg)
Stance	Biped
Where	England & France
Diet	Carnivore
Activity	Hunting & possibly scavenging
Intelligence	Medium
Named by	Rev. William Buckland
When named	1824
Order	Saurischia (Lizard-hipped)
Type	Theropoda, Tetanurae, Carnosauria

Late Cretaceous	99–66
Early Cretaceous	144–99
Late Jurassic	159–144
Middle Jurassic	190–159
Early Jurassic	205–190
Late Triassic	227–205
Middle Triassic	242–227
Early Triassic	251–242

Spinosaurus

Pronounced: *spy-noh-SAW-ruhs*

The first and best example of *Spinosaurus* was discovered and named by Ernst Stromer in 1912 in Egypt. Unfortunately, the skeleton became another casualty of bombing during World War II. Further partial discoveries were made in 1996. Studies of these discoveries suggest that *Spinosaurus* was the largest carnivorous dinosaur, longer even than either *Giganotosaurus* or *Tyrannosaurus rex*. It had a long snout of about 3 feet (1 m), similar to that of a crocodile. *Spinosaurus* takes its name from its most distinctive feature: a row of bony spines, over 5 feet (1.5 m) long, attached to the backbone. These were covered with skin to form a "sail," which was used to regulate the temperature of the dinosaur and also for display purposes. The shape of the snout and teeth, and the discovery of a fish bone among the teeth, indicates that *Spinosaurus* fed mainly off fish. Surprisingly, *Spinosaurus* was not well adapted for swimming or diving in water despite its dependence on an aquatic lifestyle. *Spinosaurus* would have most likely scavenged or hunted dinosaurs to get additional food.

Statistics

Meaning	Spiny Lizard
When	Cretaceous
Time	112–94 million years ago
Max length	55 feet (17 m)
Max height	22 feet (6.75 m)
Max weight	19,850 pounds (9,000 kg)
Stance	Biped
Where	Egypt & Morocco
Diet	Carnivore
Activity	Hunting
Intelligence	Medium
Named by	Ernst Stromer
When named	1915
Order	Saurischia (Lizard-hipped)
Type	Theropoda, Tetanurae, Carnosauria

Timeline
Million Years Ago

Late Cretaceous
99-66

Early Cretaceous
144-99

Late Jurassic
159-144

Middle Jurassic
190-159

Early Jurassic
205-190

Late Triassic
227-205

Middle Triassic
242-227

Early Triassic
251-242

Tyrannosaurus rex

Pronounced: *tuh-ran-uh-SAW-ruhs rex*

Tyrannosaurus rex is the most famous of all the dinosaurs. For a long time it was thought to be the largest meat-eating dinosaur ever, until *Giganotosaurus* and *Spinosaurus* were discovered. Both of these dinosaurs were longer than *T. rex*, but not as heavy. The skull of *T. rex* was large, with strong jaws containing curved, serrated teeth up to 6 inches (15 cm) long and with a huge bite. It had powerful legs and arms, though the arms were very short. Its arms had two-clawed hands for gripping and holding prey. *T. rex* had a good sense of smell and could run at up to 25 miles (45 km) per hour to ambush and kill prey. It may have scavenged as well. Fossilized dung, known as coprolites, show that its main diet was plant-eating dinosaurs, such as *Triceratops* and duck-billed dinosaurs. *T. rex* had a scaly, reptilian skin with possibly some small feathers around the neck. *T. rex* did not roar. Its call was a mixture of that of a booming bird and a crocodile, but much lower.

Statistics

Meaning	Tyrant Lizard King
When	Late Cretaceous
Time	71–65 million years ago
Max length	42 feet (12.8 m)
Max height	18 feet (5.5 m)
Max weight	21, 600 pounds (9,800 kg)
Stance	Biped
Where	United States (Colorado, Montana, Wyoming, Texas) & Canada (Alberta, Saskatchewan)
Diet	Carnivore
Activity	Hunting and/or scavenging
Intelligence	Medium
Named by	Henry Fairfield Osborn
When named	1905
Order	Saurischia (Lizard-hipped)
Type	Theropoda, Tetanurae, Coelurosauria

Timeline
Million Years Ago

Late Cretaceous
99–66

Early Cretaceous
144–99

Late Jurassic
159–144

Middle Jurassic
190–159

Early Jurassic
205–190

Late Triassic
227–205

Middle Triassic
242–227

Early Triassic
251–242

The Largest Carnivore

Spinosaurus may have been longer than *T. Rex*, but it hasn't been found to be the same kind of fierce hunter. Scientists have studied fossils of *Spinosaurus* and concluded its body parts were adapted for eating mostly fish!

GLOSSARY

ancestor: an animal in the past from which another animal developed

flexible: able to be bent

fossil: the remains or traces of plants and animals from the past

impression: something made by pressing on a surface, such as footprints

jaws: the bones of the head that hold the teeth

sauropod: a group of dinosaurs from the Jurassic and Cretaceous that walked on all fours, had a long neck and tail, and a small head

scavenger: an animal that commonly eats carrion, or dead animals, left behind by other animals

serrated: having a row of small points or teeth along the side like a saw

theropod: a group of carnivorous dinosaurs that walked on two feet

World War II: a war fought mainly in Europe and Asia from 1939 to 1945

FOR MORE INFORMATION

Books

Dinosaur Atlas. Washington, D.C.: National Geographic, 2021.

Terp, Gail. *Taking Care of Your T. Rex*. Mankato, MN: Black Rabbit Books, 2022.

Weakland, Mark. *Two-Legged, Meat-Eating Dinosaurs: Ranking Their Speeds, Strength, and Smarts*. North Mankato, MN: Bolt, 2020.

Websites

Dinosaur Facts
www.dkfindout.com/us/dinosaurs-and-prehistoric-life/dinosaurs/
Find out about other kinds of dinosaurs on this interactive site.

Tyrannosaurus rex
kids.nationalgeographic.com/animals/prehistoric/facts/tyrannosaurus-rex
Read more about this famous dinosaur here!

INDEX